Quiet Things Quiet Places

LEONA KOEHN NICHOLS

"Your story is our priority"

LitPrime Solutions
21250 Hawthorne Blvd
Suite 500, Torrance, CA 90503
www.litprime.com
Phone: 1-800-981-9893

Published by LitPrime Solutions   03/31/2022

ISBN: 978-1-955177-86-3(sc)
ISBN: 978-1-955177-87-0(e)

Contents

Everyday Observations

Nature

Faith

Family

Christmas Joy

Poems that tell a story

Introduction

My love for poetry was a legacy handed down from my mother. The book she treasured, entitled Golden Thoughts from the Great Writers, was one I carried out to my swing to read as I slowly moved back and forth. I'm sure I loved it as much for the elegant prints scattered through the book and its gold edging and beautiful cover as I did its poems, which were mostly beyond me. However, I was introduced to Longfellow's famous "Life is real, life is earnest, and the grave is not its goal; dust thou art to dust returnest was not spoken of the soul." That stuck, for some reason.

A more readable book for a child was A Child's Garden of Verses, which had poems designed for the young child. One of my favorites there was "My Shadow," which I memorized, as well as several others.

But it was my sixth grade teacher, Mrs. Kemper, who really gave me the love for poetry I have carried all my life. She had us get our coats and lunch boxes, sit at our desks, and memorize poetry the last fifteen minutes of each day. By the end of the year we had memorized twenty of more poems, many of them lengthy. My favorite here was "The House with Nobody in It."

I began to write my own thoughts down fairly early, but those are now lost. However, I began writing and keeping my thoughts somewhere in my thirties and forties. After I became a teacher in my early fifties, the poetry unit in my English classes was the most important unit we completed. I convinced all my students that every one could write poetry of some sort, and whether it rhymed or not was inconsequential. I hope somewhere they are still writing.

The Little Girl Inside

"As long as I can skip," I said
"I'll never be old."
And so I skipped to the mailbox
And back again
While the May flowers nodded their heads.

But when November comes
And my legs get shaky
And the mailbox seems further away
I know the little girl inside
Will keep on skipping—
That's just the way she is.

Everyday Observations

I Love Quiet Things

I love quiet things, quiet places
Walks in the shadowed, silent woods
Away from the noise of busy traffic.

But the world I live in
Makes many sounds—
Some so loud I cover my ears
And wait 'til the turmoil fades.

Still, there are sounds I like—
The cheerful song of the mocking bird
As he greets the morning light.
The distant wail of the coyote calling,
Calling to each other in the night.
The drone of tractors
Working in the field across the road
The deep bass croak of a bullfrog
Sitting on a rock in the fish pond.

And then there are sounds I love—
The pitter patter of a gentle spring rain,
The happy sound of a child talking
To her dolls or stuffed animals,

The gentle mew of kittens hungry
For their mamma's milk—
The hummingbirds, wings awhirl
As they nose-drive into flower petals.

But the best sound of all is only
In my memory—the sound of my
Precious baby, cooing to herself
As she wakes in her bassinette
Ready to begin her day with a smile.

Ode to Life

Spotless and clean as the fresh dewy morning,
Refreshing and pure as a high mountain stream;
Sturdy and strong as a tree reaching upward
Shining and clear as the dancing sunbeam.

Tasty and nourishing as bread from the oven,
Fragrant and sweet as the breath of a flower;
Soaring to heights as on wings of an eagle,
Bright as a star at the dark midnight hour.

Life is a gift we receive from the Giver
Ours to experience, to share and to live;
Rich in variety, it finds expression
Not in holding it close, but in learning to give.

Hearts that are hungry need bread from our ovens,
Eyes that are dim need the dancing sunbeam;
Spirits that droop need the flight of an eagle
Calling them up to the heights once again.

Oh, let us savor the sweet joy of living,
Tasting, absorbing the beauty we see;
Never complaining when duty is pressing,
Content to serve others, to feel, and to be.

Life is not made for continual excitement,
Hurry and scurry and worry and strife;
O, let us taste of the joys of contentment
As with thankful heart, we truly live life.

Faces

I see it in the faces of the young—
The vacant eyes that tug so at my heart,
The pain of severed families. The sound
Of hurting children, crying in the night.

I see it in the aimlessness of feet
That follow diverse paths that lead nowhere
A generation whose limits are removed,
The freedom they reach out for just a fake.

I see it in the faces of the old
The shattered dreams of youth a memory
Pulled from their grasp by cruel hands of fate
That rob the sweetness from declining years.

I see it, and I reach out with my heart
Choosing to share the pain, to share the tears,
Believing that the power of love will bring
The gift of healing and the light of hope.

If I Could, I Would ...

Give out smiles for every face
All disappointment I'd erase
Make all little children safe
And see "happy" on every face
Let every mother know she's loved
Let each dad know he's admired
Solve the problems in this land
Share with all a helping hand.

To the poor I'd ease the strain
To the sick relieve the pain
To the sad I'd bring some joy
Blessings for each girl and boy.

Yes, I wish so much I could
Help each do just what they should
Kindness spread throughout the land
For God and country firmly stand.

But I can't make each person good
Make them do all that they should
I can only speak for me
I can be what I should be
I can do what I should do
What you do depends on you.

The Fleeting Years

Where have they gone—
Days of relentless busyness
The nights, with fevered bodies,
Skin too hot and cheeks too bright
Cradled in my arms, as we
Awaited morning light?

Where have they gone—
The muddy footprints on the floor
The outline crust of
Peanut butter bread
Discarded on the counter top—
The lumpy bed?

Where have they gone?
The nights of anxious waiting
'Til car lights shined on window panes
Releasing nameless fears
So that I crawled once more into my bed
To sleep in thankfulness?

Where have they gone—
The fleeting days, the rushing years
The pleasure and the pain they brought
So lightly etched in memory—
Some still vivid, some forgot
That fill each mother's heart?

A Friend Concealed

I have a friend concealed behind
The curtain of your eyes;
And though I try to peer inside
I only can surmise
You choose to stay hidden within
Not wanting to reveal
The "you" I want so much to know
To share the things you feel.

I read the sign out on the gate,
"By invitation only."
I cannot enter, I must wait
Although the waiting's lonely.
I cannot force an entrance
Into that inner place
And if the invitation comes
I'll read it on your face.
Sometimes I think I see a spark
To light my waiting fire—
Sometime I'll share that secret place—
That is my heart's desire.

Temptation

Two kingdoms rage within my breast
Two rulers seek to draw
My loyalties unto themselves
To bind me to their law.

And I, how can I hear the truth
In their tempestuous shouting
I choose, and then I choose again—
Still I am left with doubting.

My head says "no," my heart says "yes,"
Why I must go on trying
To find some reason to it all—
Why is my heart still crying?

Two kingdoms rage within my breast
They fight to gain control;
Where is the strength by which I stand?
Which one will buy my soul?

Hard Work

Making decisions is hard work
I make them every day.
I choose the path my feet will walk
Both in my work and play.

Sometimes I make a bad mistake
And I pay dearly then—
For consequences surely come
I never know just when.

But even though they're hard, not easy
I'm glad I have the chance
To ponder, choose, my life's direction
To sing my own song and dance.

Dreamer or Schemer?

Yep, I am a dreamer,
An out and out schemer,
I want what I want when I want it;
I'll work day and night
If I have to I'll fight
But I'll try and I'll try 'til I get it.

I don't sit in the summer
And wonder and wonder
If something good's comin' my way
I go out and I'll get it
I'll grab it and sit on it
And I'll work for it all night and day.

Yes, I am persistent
And downright resistant
To waiting for luck to find me—
I figger I'd better
Get off of my "sitter"
And chase down the "want" that I see.

Now this is my story
I can't claim the glory
For bein' an ornery 'ole cuss
My dad was hard-workin'
He never tried shirkin'
And from the same cloth I am cut.

The Towering Tree

Tall it stands, with leafy arms stretched toward the sky
Compelling my gaze upward as I pass by,
Going the same way, day after day
Down the busy street, and on my way
To face the stresses life will bring
The challenges, problems, everything
That is a part of the life I live
A life that requires me daily to give.

Yet, every day my eyes are lifted
By the giant tree, and my heart is gifted
By its strength and beauty, just standing there
As if to say, "Yes, I'm still here—
The storms have come and the winds have blown
But I'm still here, standing alone—
Like me, put your roots down deep in the soil
And build a foundation that in the toil
Of everyday living will hold you firm—"
Yes, the tree is a teacher from which I learn.

That tree is a legend of hope and style
I let go of my frown and I start to smile
And say "Hey, towering tree, keep standing there
Through the mists of life, you help me see clear;
For storms will come, and storms will go,
But you and I will stand firm, I know."

Her Way

She walked out of the house,
Slammed the door and
Walked quickly down the street,
Her anger pushing her on.

It was one time too many—
She couldn't take it anymore
Her parents treated her like a child
Who couldn't make her own decisions.

Couldn't they see she wasn't a baby anymore
Now that she was fifteen and a half
She would choose her own friends—
Live her own life, be her own person.

She hurried down the street, going
Nowhere—anywhere—just away somewhere,
Choosing her own life, her destiny.
A place where no one told her "No!"

A car came screeching around the corner
Someone saw her, stopped, yelled, "Get in!"
Good! It seemed somebody wanted her—
But no one ever saw her again.

Soliloquy at Dusk

It's nearly dark—
The dusk settles in and
The mountains really are purple—
"For purple mountains, majesty..."
I loved singing that song in the third grade.
It's time to go in,
Fix a little supper, and ...
Remember when the kids were small?
They never wanted to stop playing
Even when it got dark.
I'm really tired...
Time to put this pruning shear away—
How beautiful those lilacs are!
Is it ever really spring until the lilacs bloom?
That darn cat looks pregnant again
I should have had her spayed, but
How the kids loved those baby kittens...
Finding them, counting how many she'd had this time–
Oh well... the kids are grown, but
What darling babies they each were...

I'd hold them, staring at the mirror,
Trying so hard to fix their images
Indelibly in my mind–
Six tiny humans, eyes searching my face,
Fingers curled around mine
Perfect babies, each a symbol of our love,
Irrevocable evidence of the continuity of life.
It's nearly dark—
Time to go in—
I'm really tired,
But I think I'll stay a bit and smell the lilacs.

The Boy on the Swing

The boy on the swing is always there
Swinging on the park swing, often high in the air,
And each day I wonder, as I see him fly
Through the air on a swing, shooting up to the sky.

The boy on the swing is a mystery
The reason he's there I really can't see;
With his backpack beside him there on the grass
He vigorously swings as I'm driving past.

I wonder, is it freedom he seeks in the park?
Is he putting off schedules? Is he out on a lark?
Does he love school, or hate it, does he swing to forget
That life has its challenges, some he's already met?

I love seeing him there, the boy on the swing—
There is something about him that makes my heart sing;
As I drive by each morning, my heart too will soar—
If he's still there tomorrow, I'll see him once more.

No Longer There

The boy on the swing is no longer there
He's not swinging slowly, nor high in the air;
It seems he has found other things to do
There are other activities he now must pursue.

Of course, I still wonder, as I drive by
And my prayer for him comes as a sort of a sigh
Lord, bless the boy who has drifted away;
Help him still to find shining joy in his day.

I know that he's older, and maybe he feels
That a swing in the park is now no big deal;
Perhaps he has found new ways to have fun
He may feel that his "swinging days" now are all done.

You know him, Lord, even though I don't
You know his name, and even though I won't
Even know where he comes from, or why he was there;
I'm glad for a short time my life he did share.

We never know, when we see someone new,
Should we stop, perhaps smile and say "How do you do?"
But there's one thing that's certain, as through life we go—
We can pray that God's love on each child He'll bestow

Little Girl, Big Ocean

A little girl, a great big ocean
Waves pushing up on the beach
Sand for digging, sand for playing
More sand than anyone could need.

So I remember the days of childhood
The joy I found by the sea
Just a small little child by a big, big ocean
Fearing the waves would swallow me.

And still today I find great pleasure
In visiting the ocean so vast;
It's so big only God could have made it
And I hope it will always last.

Just a little girl and a great big ocean
In memory I see her still—
Running and playing, laughing and screaming—
I loved it then, and I always will.

Foolish Heart

My heart is so irrational—
I think it never really listens to my brain
Foolishly, it attaches itself tenaciously
To the most unlikely things
And people
My heart is like a little child
Who answers "why?" with "Just because"
No reason—
Just the heart speaking
Creating its own truth
Disregarding reality.

Sometimes I wish my heart would listen up!
For, like a child, it frequently gets hurt.
It's wounded by the most unlikely things
And people.
The brain is quick to scream,
"I told you so...
When will you learn to listen?

Nature

Spring Moves

Spring creeps into my consciousness
quietly, secretly, persistent as
a green garden snake, looking for
sunshine and space, weary of
Old constricting skin.

Spring gains momentum in my senses
as an avalanche down a mountain
greedy for power and motion
impelled to explore new territory
beyond itself.

Spring bursts into my perception
like a running child, overcome
with the excitement of his world,
eager to shout to the heavens
what he cannot contain.

Spring explodes all over my spirit
like a torrent of swift water
tearing away old limitations
uncovering fresh ideas
bringing new life.

Camping

Hearing the wind through the tall, pine trees
Humming a lullaby;
A blanket of stars, hanging so low
That you feel you could reach the sky.

Clear, cold streams that ramble away,
Bubbling merrily on
From shadowed pool to rushing brooks,
Singing a happy song.

Mountains whose peaks reach up to the sky
Like monuments so tall—
The evidence of the Creator's hand
In the grandeur of it all.

Deep blue skies like a canopy spread,
To hold everything in place;
While over the hills, like scattered jewels
Wild flowers show smiling face.

And where does one go to fill his soul
With the beauty of nature grand?
Why, up in the mountains, to a quiet place,
Where I have been camping, my friend!

The Mountain Stream

The little stream meandered through the meadow
As though it had a special place to go—
A mission that it needed to accomplish
The pace it chose deliberate and slow.

Around the rocks and through the shallow places
Its gentle song was hardly heard at all
Above the whisper of the lofty tree-tops
Above the distant trill of the robin's call.

So gently flows the stream of life within us
In quiet times and quiet places still—
The times when we sit silent in His Presence,
The times when we surrender to His will.

Then words of praise just like the bubbling freshet
Spring up within our hearts in glad surprise
And like the little stream we see our mission
To lift sad hearts and help them to arise.

Tall Granite Peaks

The morning sun touches the tall granite peaks
With the message that daybreak has come;
The darkness has vanished in light of the sun
And the shadows have slithered away.

I gaze at the mountains so somber and still
As their peaks break the azure blue sky,
And I look at myself, just five foot four—
Compared to those peaks, what am I!

"What is man that You are mindful of him?"
Your creation overpowers us all!
The grandeur of nature is beyond all compare,
While we are so puny and small.

God, help us to see just how helpless we are,
How we need You in every way;
Our strength is so small, we depend upon You
Be our strength as we walk day by day.

Life's Changing Seasons

A winter landscape outside my window
Is just a reminder that seasons change
That nothing in life is permanent
And life has its moments of pain.
There will be some disappointments,
But these cannot last too long
And "joy does come in the morning,"
It comes with a burst of song.

When autumn shows its fall colors
And soon the fierce north winds will blow
Don't give up and be disheartened,
Another season will come and go.
And though you shiver when cold comes
Or you snuggle besides the warm fire
Though the air outside is chilly
Spring may bring you your heart's desire.

For life is much like the seasons
We go through good times and bad—
Still, we look ahead to the future
To a time when we'll be less sad.
When the sun shines a little bit warmer
And the daffodils peep through the earth—
Just lift up your eyes to the heavens
And smile for all you're worth!

The Merced River

The Merced River is always there—
Its ruffled surface quietly concealing
The long-held secrets of its shadowed past,
Tracing its journey down an ancient course,
Confined within its banks, no longer free,
It moves with measured feet where it must go;
Contained by human minds and concrete dams,
Its power harnessed to a measured flow.

The river is always there—
But once it knew another life:
Wild as a mountain lion it moved
Down California's hills, across her plains,
In spring, wildly flowing, unfettered, devouring all
That lay along its banks, until the time
Its force was spent, retreating once again,
Its strength depleted, lost in melted snow.

The river is still there, and as a child
I played within its shallows, cool and clear,
Dreaming of ancient peoples, vanished then,
Who lived along its streams, beneath its oaks.
Once native Californians walked these banks
Their children, just as I, had known its joys;
Sustained by flowing waters, even then—
The river is always there.

The Winter Sentinel

Outside the window, like a brown sentinel
It stands guard, holding its position stiffly
Against the blustery, stinging wind
Its myriad branches stand with military precision
And silent dignity, pointing to the wintry sky.

The leaves have fallen, but hidden within
The brown, barren casing is the promise
Whispered within the silence of every twig—
Spring is coming! I hold the secret inside,
So deep inside. But I cannot long contain it—
Spring will burst forth
With startling, brilliant green
And I will triumph once again
Over winter.

Sonnets, just for fun! Teaching Shakespearian
sonnets was always fun (for me) in my
English classes. Here are a few I wrote.

When In Disgrace

When in disgrace with fortune and men's eyes
I take myself to task for all I've done
With all the stupid things, I realize
My brain was just checked out from sun to sun.
Was I asleep, or was I just insane?
How will I ever know? I can't recall
Why I would blessed common sense disdain
For some lame proverb found upon my wall
O, mercy me! I just don't get the drift
Or why I thought intelligent design
Would skip me like a speeding sailing ship
And leave me loony for a length of time.
And yet, I cannot truly say that all is lost
For surely kindness in my lap was tossed.

Sonnet 10

If I could wish for one delight below
Upon this earth, this place of our abode
I'd wish for love, that I could fully know
The joy of sharing life along the road.
If I compose a song of love divine
And feel the sun and hear the songbird sing
I'd know that deep within this heart of mine
The cord of love we share will pleasure bring.
If I could send my love out on the wind
To circle 'round your heart with fragrance sweet
And every thought of sadness to rescind
And garlands spread of beauty at your feet
Then would I know our hearts would beat as one
Contentment would be ours at set of sun.

Sonnet 19

You were just a baby when you came
Into my life with promise yet unknown
I looked into your eyes and saw the same
Delight without a single smile yet shown
I watched you grow, I treasured every step
You were a jewel far beyond compare
I watched as little feet became adept
I shared each waking moment with a prayer.
Oh, what a gift God placed within my hands
So undeserved, so matchless, so sublime
A gift of heaven to these shores of sand
As graciously You made this new child mine.
Oh, who can understand the joy of heaven
Unless to him a little child is given.

Sonnet 23

When in the presence of a faithful friend
I find that all my worries fly away
And I find peace and joy without an end
As we recall the pleasures of the day.
We talk of places we have sometimes been
And places that we hope sometime to be
We mine these treasures in our minds, and then
We fancy what someday we hope to see.
When suddenly we find that we must part
That we must leave and go our separate ways
And even though it grieves our souls and heart
We know that we shall meet in better days.
O what a joy it is to have a friend
So kind and true until the very end.

When I Consider

When I consider how my life is spent
How quickly time has flown from day to day
And I have wandered stumbling on my way
My youth and strength diminished as I went.
The talents that I thought to be my own
Were lent to me only to honor Him
So graciously He paid for all my sin
And shed His blood my nature to atone.
And so I see 'twas all but just a gift
My poverty a plague I could not hide
And seeing thus my emptiness inside
His love has healed the cataclysmic rift.
And so the debt I owe cannot be done
In one short life until my race is run.

Faith

Tradition

And the Pharisees spake and said unto Him,
"Why walk your disciples not in
The traditions of the elders? We hold
Such conduct to be a sin.
For they eat their bread with unwashed hands
As the heathen and sinner do;
Defiling themselves by the careless neglect
Of the law they are subject to."

But Jesus said, "Ye hypocrites!
Though you honor God with your words,
'Your hearts are all afar from Him
And you seek not the things of the Lord.
For in laying aside the commandments of God
In vain do you worship Him.
You hold instead the traditions of men
And pridefully follow them.
What do you seek to follow, my friends,
As into His presence you go?
Do you empty yourselves of foolish pride

And the wisdom of men here below?
For God is not pleased with the washing of hands,
He seeks for the hungry heart—
The heart that is crying and knows its need
To be cleansed in its innermost part.

Though many and good were the ways of the past
Tradition does not make them holy—
And God will reject our proud, pious hearts
And will welcome the one who is lowly.

I Will Trust Jesus

I will trust Jesus, just for today
Give Him my hand as I walk in His way
Staying close by Him, feeling Him near,
Yielding completely, in faith and not fear.

I will trust Jesus to fill all my needs,
The lily He clothes and the sparrow He feeds;
He loves me much more than the birds of the air,
How securely I rest as I'm safe in His care.

I will trust Jesus to teach me His Word,
To open the Scriptures, revealing my Lord;
Lifting, enlightening, feeding my soul
With nourishing Bread of Life, making me whole.

I will trust Jesus to keep me from sin,
Washing me, cleansing me, keeping me clean,
Using my body His temple to be,
Forming the image of Jesus in me.

I will trust Jesus to fill me with power,
Strength for my weakness in every dark hour,
Comfort in sorrow, courage in pain,
Restored by His Spirit, again and again.

I will trust Jesus to guide me each day,
Lovingly, gently, not letting me stray,
In every decision I'll seek for His will,
Believing that He will His promise fulfill.

I will trust Jesus, O bless His dear Name,
For O, He is worthy, His grace I'll proclaim.
Faithful and loving, tender and true,
I'll praise Him and worship Him all my life through.

Through Jesus I'm Free

Salvation through Jesus, we sing and we say,
There's naught but His blood that can take sins away."
But then, just because we can't grasp that it's free,
We add this and that as requirements, you see.

"Just faith in His blood, just in Jesus alone—
It can't be that simple our sins to atone;
No, you must do this, put this on, take that off—
You must not go there, somebody might scoff!

Come, let's make a rule, so we know what to do—
How long should your beard be, what color your shoe.
What car should you drive, what job should you hold,
Don't bother to pray, just do as you're told!

Until finally you're loaded with do's and with don'ts,
Your mind is all weary with shalls and with won'ts
For our Savior has come, all your burdens to bear,
If you'll yield him your life and let Him take your care.

He'll give you His Spirit to live in your heart,
He'll lead you and guide you and never depart;
Just trust Him, relax, all your turmoil is through,
He'll lead you so gently in what you should do.

Yes, Christ made us free, therefore let us BE free,
Not a license to sin, but rather to be
Conformed to His likeness, like Jesus, God's Son,
Born of His Spirit, by love all made one.

Living each moment beneath His control,
Safe in His keeping, mind, body, and soul.
O, praise Him and thank Him, so loving is He,
He died on the cross that we might go free.

"Stand fast therefore in the liberty wherein Christ has
made us free." Galatians 5:1

Communion

How strange to know that the great God of Heaven,
Creator of the vast worlds still unknown;
Immense beyond the limits of our reason
Our earth is but the footstool of His throne.
A God who spoke and oceans flowed together,
Whose thought brought forth the moon, the stars, the sun;
Yet He fashioned for Himself a finite creature
With whom His Spirit might in love commune.

How can I grasp the depth of condescension
`That God should dane to come and visit man;
That in the cool of day, as once with Adam,
His Spirit seeks me out where 'ere I am.
And so I walk with God along a brooklet,
I sit with Him upon a meadow green:
I see His hand in every tree and pebble,
I feel His presence in the sunlight gleam.
And as He comes He fills my soul with singing,
He meets the deepest needs within my heart;
And as our spirits flow in sweet communion,

I am of Him, and He of me, a part.
Yet, when I walk the dry and thirsty desert,
And though I feel alone at times, and sad,
I know that He will come again to bless me,
And in His fellowship my heart is glad.

My Gifts

I give you Love, O God of my Salvation
The same stream which now flows to you
Returns but to its source. For I can give
You only that which first You gave to me.
I give you Love.

I give you Praise, O God of my Salvation
Praise through the limits of frail lips and
Shallow understanding. And yet,
With quiet adoration, with awe-struck heart,
I give you Praise.

I give you Joy, O God of my Salvation
For in some way, unfathomable to me,
The simple, childlike trust of my response to you
Fills you with singing and delight.
I give you Joy.

These are my Gifts, O God of my Salvation;
Gifts of the heart, and wrapped in shining gratitude;
I stretch my hands to you, my face turned upward,
I give you freely all I have to give.
I give myself.

Upright and Just

(Thoughts drawn from Moses' song, Deut. 32)

God's gracious Words flow over me,
Like rain from a mellow sky;
I drink them in with a thirsty heart,
And O, how they satisfy!

A faithful God who does no wrong
Upright and just is He;
And in my weakness He is strong
His grace my only plea.

How foolish and unwise are we
To doubt our Sovereign Lord;
Come! Bow our hearts to worship Him
Together in one accord.

O let us sing His glorious praise
Loudly we will proclaim;
The greatness of our God of love—
I lift His Holy Name!
(Can be sung to melody of Glory Be To Our Great God)

Isaiah 53

A Man of sorrows and acquainted with grief,
A suffering Savior was He;
And we hid, as it were, our faces from Him
In our blindness, refused to see.

And so we despised Him and turned Him away
Our esteem we withheld from His Name;
Yet He bore our sorrows and carried our grief,
And He carried our sin and our shame.

But we thought Him stricken and smitten of God,
We judged Him afflicted and sore;
And in Him we saw no comliness
No beauty that we should adore.

Yet it was for us that He suffered alone,
For us were laid stripes on His back;
And for our transgressions His wounds He bore,
That we might have no lack.

For though we like sheep have all gone astray,
And have turned everyone to his own,
Upon Him was laid our iniquity,
Being sinless, for sin to atone.

As a lamb to the slaughter He went to the cross,
As a sheep before shearers is dumb;
So He suffered in silence, crying out not at all,
But the look in His eyes pleaded "Come."

Yet it pleased our God to bruise Him
And to make Him an offering for sin;
That through suffering there might be salvation,
And by His death we might enter in.

For me He was bruised, and for you, my friend,
For all men was the pain that He bore;
For us was despised and rejected and mocked,
Must He suffer for us even more?

For if we refuse to accept His great love,
And uncaring, we turn Him away—
Then what will we say, as we stand before God,
In judgment upon that Great Day?

Freedom With Him

We live in the Land of the Shadow of Death
Death nips at our heels each day
But light that pierces the shadows has come
And has driven our fears away.

For the Shadow of Death cannot conceal
The powerful Light that shines through
A Light of healing, a Light of hope
Restoring and making us new.

For the Shadow is just an illusion, you know
To separate us from our Lord
Who has made the ultimate sacrifice
And has given us life through His Word.

How great is the grace of our Loving Lord
Saving us from the death of this land
Preparing us for the moment of truth
When in His Presence we stand.

Oh, let us rejoice in the love He has shown
And freely to others, let's give
The news of redemption and freedom to all
That forever with Him we may live.

Preparing the Bride

You've broken the barriers down, my Lord,
You've made every wall to fall;
You've brought us together, under Your Name,
You've caused us to come at Your call.

The churches we've built to ourselves, my Lord,
To glorify us, not You;
Have all grown empty and weak and dry,
With no power to carry us through.

But You're raising up for Yourself a church
A beautiful Bride to be:
Free from the spots and wrinkles of sin,
Clothed in Your purity.

And you've called us together in unity,
You've given us work to do:
We are one in spirit, one in heart,
And one in our purpose for You.

O. strengthen us now as your bride, dear Lord,
As daughters before you we stand;
We're part of Your kingdom, bearing Your name,
And spreading Your truth through the land.

O, let us shine forth Your glory, my Lord
Aglow with your Spirit divine;
And as we go down from this mountain, my Lord,
Just cause our faces to shine!

God's In Control

We hurry and scurry and rush about,
We go in for a moment, and then we go out,
We fret and we fume, we simmer and stew
There's no time to enjoy, there's just too much to do.

How silly we are, to race and to run,
So busy and anxious, we miss all the fun
The first thing we know, our life's nearly gone
And we may collapse, but the rat race goes on.

So, stop just a moment! Just stop in your tracks.
Draw a deep breath, sit down and relax
And let sweet contentment sink deep in your soul—
And smile as you say, "Friends, God's in control!"

Today

Today is new and clean
God washed it with His love
It sparkles with His sunshine,
It smiles down from above.

It smells as fresh and sweet
As laundry on a line
It's measured out in minutes
A jewel set in time.

Oh, breathe it deep and savor
The joy that is today
A blessing without measure,
Unique in every way.

So, give this day to Jesus
Don't dirty it with sin
You'll be, when it is over
Just a little more like Him.

The Shepherd

How often times we read, "The Lord's my shepherd,"
How comforting to feel we're in His care;
We love to be His sheep, and in Him trusting,
We know He gently keeps us from the snare.

"I shall not want," O what a precious promise
What 'ere my needs I know He will supply;
In meadows green, and by the waters placid,
He maketh me, His willing sheep, to lie.

"He maketh me to lie"—say, what is this, Lord?
You want me to lie down upon this bed?
You want me to be here, when I would rather
Be busy with Thy vineyard needs instead?

He makes me to lie down—I have no doubt, Lord,
'Tis something you have planned, for I
Would choose a different way to do Thy bidding—
I would not choose upon this bed to lie.

"He maketh me to lie," Lord there's a reason
And sometimes in the darkened mirror of life,
I catch a fleeting glimpse of heavenly vision;
Of faith that gives me victory o're strife.

"He makes me to lie down," and so you have, Lord.
Now help me too, that I might fill my place;
For I am weak, and often times in pain, Lord;
Yet for my needs, I know thou givest grace.

And so, dear Lord, I'll lie here where you've put me;
Yours is the hand that fashioned this design.
And even though I do not know the future,
I'll simply put my trusting hand in Thine.

The Sacrifice

Oh, Lord, I come in deep contrition
Before your cross
Bringing my failure and my rash ambition
My sin and dross
I cannot stand before a God so holy
My shame is great
How can I plead for undeserved forgiveness
I simply wait—
The cross! An instrument of execution
Designed for me
My sin has sentenced me to die in anguish—
And then I see
That you have chosen to lay stretched upon it
You took my place
You took the pain I so deserved and dreaded
All my disgrace.
O, Cross of Calvary—I fall in worship
At your dear feet
In humble adoration, then I hear
"It is complete!

In death I paid the costly price
You could not pay
The freedom you could never purchase
I gave away
You are set free—forgiven
My precious child
It is upon this rugged cross that we
Are reconciled."

The Call

Once a man walked this earth
Through His life, from His birth
He became all that a man could ever be;
Healed the sick, cured the lame
By the power of His name,
To the sin-sick gently called, O follow Me!

Follow me, follow Me,
On the sand, by the sea,
Where I walked, and where I taught the hungry crowd
Follow me, up the hill
To a cross, where I still,
Speak to all the weary world, O follow Me.

Along the shores by the sea,
Of the sparkling Galilee,
There were fisherman called Peter, James and John;
Then one day Jesus came, and He called them each by
name,
Saying unto them, "O come and follow me."

Still He calls us today,

In the cities, by the way,

In whatever path of life that you might be;

Leave your fears, leave your strife,

I will give eternal life,

Open up your heart and come and follow me.

Living With Jesus

Walking with Jesus, day after day,
Learning to love Him, to trust and obey,
Drawing much closer to His tender heart
Leaving the cares that would drive you apart.

Listening to Jesus, learning to pray,
Sharing your thoughts with Him, day after day;
Gaining new strength for the trials you meet,
Hearing His voice as you sit at His feet.

Looking to Jesus, so that you might be
Conformed more and more to His image, you see;
Changed by His power as you gaze at His face,
Reflecting His likeness, receiving His grace.

Depending on Jesus to meet all your needs,
Obediently walking the path that He leads;
Resisting the forces of darkness and fear,
Trusting His promise that He's always near.

Resting in Jesus as onward you go,
Letting His peace to your heart ever flow;
Knowing the future holds nothing to dread,
Living with Jesus, what joy lies ahead!

A Friend to Sinners

It wasn't with the rich or the respected
It wasn't with the high society
It wasn't with the "in bunch," that Jesus went to lunch
Nor with the Doctors of Divinity.

Cho: But Jesus was a friend, a friend of sinners
He sat at meat with those who were unclean
He said, "It's not the well who need the doctor,
Nor the righteous do I call to come to me."

The Pharisees oft criticized the Master
When He spoke of mercy meaning more than law
To the proud he pronounced many woes,
and he stepped on respected toes,
But those who felt their need His love did draw.

Rivers of Living Water

On the day of the feast Jesus stood up and said,
"If any man thirst let him come
Let him come unto me and drink, freely drink
Of the fountain that never runs dry."

Cho: For he who believes as the Scripture has said,
Out of his innermost part,
Shall flow rivers of waters that flow, freely flow,
Bringing life to the dry thirsty heart.

Jesus spoke of the Spirit that all should receive
Who believe in the true Son of God
For the promise is given to all who believe
Just for asking by faith in His Word.

There's a well springing forth of pure water within
And it flows out to touch every one
And it springs from the fountain that's deep in my heart
It's the Spirit of the Life-giving Son.

Step Out in Faith

Peter was a fisherman, on the sea of Galilee
With an old rowboat and a fishing net
That's where he liked to be.
Then one night in a stormy gale,
He looked out on the sea,
And there was Jesus, walking on the water,
Saying, "Peter, come to me."

Peter stepped out of that boat, and he wasn't afraid at all,
Until he looked at the great big waves,
Then he began to fall;
"Save me, Lord", he cried so loud,
And Jesus caught him up,
And said, "O you of little faith,
O wherefore did you doubt?"

We've set sail on a little boat,

On the great big sea of Life

And there's plenty of waves to sink our boat,

There's hate and greed and strife;

But Jesus calls each one of us,

And He says, "Come unto me!"

So, get out of the boat and take His hand,

And you'll walk on top of the sea!

Family

A Tribute to a Beloved Brother

He walked through life with a song in his heart
A smile on his face, his eye on the mark
Of the prize of the high calling of Jesus Christ
And he lived what he believed.

He didn't have wealth or riches or fame
But you could count on the strength of his name
The truth of his word, the shake of his hand
And his outlook was honest and true.

A man is a man when he takes a firm stand
To do what is right, to live in this land
To make it a better place because he was here—
That's what makes my brother so dear.

There's not much we can say when our journey is done
But "I've fought a good fight, and the race that I've run
Has not made me famous or brought me applause
But I've lived my life for the Lord."
(For my beloved brother Gene)

My Son

I am his mother, and he is my son
And like the sound of music these words rang
In accent sweet, into my very heart;
He is of me, and I of him, a part.

I am his mother, and he is my boy
A source of testing and a source of joy
For by his life, he shows for all to see
The graces and the faults he finds in me.

I am his mother, and he is my child
And though my mother heart will oft beat wild
And I would want to shield him close to me
I dare not make him too dependent be.

And so, although my love surrounds him still
Please God, give me the courage that I will
Just let him grow, according to Thy plan...
But this I ask—Just help him be, a man.

Queen of the Kitchen Floor

This little girl, just two, who sits
upon my kitchen floor
Is Queen of all the pots and pans
She's pulled from out my drawer.

A skillet and a muffin tin
a cereal box or two,
She grins when I walk in, she knows
I'm just an old soft shoe.

Now there are those whose kingdoms reach
From shore to shining shore;
But I know one whose kingdom covers
My entire kitchen floor.

Hike Around the Lake

We walked around the lake today
A challenging hike to say the least
Some places were narrow, some were steep
We looked for a safe place to set our feet.

Three loving daughters watched carefully
To see that I didn't stumble or fall
They knew that the hike was a challenge for me
We wanted to walk with no accidents at all.

"Let me give you a helping hand," they would say
And I saw just how much like life this was
For the road that we travel is treacherous
With much to deter us or cause us to fall.

And just like life, this hike became
A contest between what is easy or hard
There are times when the sun shines, times when it rains
There are times of courage and times when you're tired.

And a helping hand means more than you know
When the path is rugged and far from smooth,
When it climbs up hill and the holes are deep
And its hard to tell which way is the truth.

So, take time to reach out with a helping hand
Take time to speak the encouraging word;
Take time to lift up a prayer of hope
As you point others gently to the Lord.
(Thanks, Micki, Bethany, Darlisa)

Demonstrated Love

He worked so hard, this man who shares my life
Each strenuous day a revelation of his heart
Poured out in sweat, to earn for us that small reward
That we turned into milk and bread and shoes.

Love was not just an empty phrase told in the night
To cast a spell that brought him his desire;
He lived love out in days of struggling toil
That brought our waiting dreams yet closer to our grasp.

He demonstrated love with drops of sweat, and yet
I never loved him more than in those moments when
His manly strength disguised with tenderness
He gently cuddled our new child.
(A tribute to my husband Willis)

To My Special Dad

When a girl has a dad who is honest and true,
Loving and faithful to carry things through
Steady and strong, on him she can depend
She's got more than a dad, he is also a friend.

When a girl has a dad who walks in the Way,
The path of our Lord, ever striving each day
To learn more of Jesus, to stay by His side
She's got more than a dad, he is also a guide.

A girl needs a dad who is gentle, yet strong,
Who clearly can see the right from the wrong,
Someone she looks up to, not perfect, but good,
A man who lives daily as other men should.

A girl needs a dad to whom she can go,
To share with and pray with when she's feeling low;
A dad who will listen, and will love her still
When the path she must follow seems to him so uphill.

I have a dad who is like all these things;
He understands when I cry, or when my heart sings
He'd like to protect me from all life's hard knocks
He'd smooth out my valleys and throw out the rocks.

Life isn't all roses, there's thorns in it too,
The fire must try us to see if we're true.
But whatever happens, of good or of bad
I praise God for giving me an extra-special Dad!

Happy Family Times

Sitting around the campfire
Recalling days of yore
Singing rounds and old songs
Sung many times before.
Watching the fire crackle
Spitting out sparks now and then—
Light reflected on faces
Talking of "way back when."

Remembering times when the children
Were small and not so brave
With darkness all around them
Only Mom and Dad could save
Hearing those strange night noises—
It could be cougars or bears
Out in the big dark forest
There were easily imagined fears.
The memories of our campfires
Are a treasure deep inside
Of families being together

Sharing family life side by side.
These were the precious dear times
Of our family growing close
Of knowing we needed each other
Of times we treasure the most.

A Family Who Loves

Show me a family who loves Jesus as Lord
I'll show you a family who lives in accord
Who finds grace to live in gentleness
Where the fracture of anger does not exist.

Show me a family whose highest desire
Is to honor their Lord, and where burns the fire
Of sharing the faith that is precious to them
To draw others to God and away from sin.

Show me a family who are servants indeed
To the lonely, the sad, and to all those in need
Who give of themselves, whether little or much
And the call on their lives shines as bright as a torch.

Show me a family whose joy is the Word
Whose desire is to draw always close to the Lord
And to hide His Word deeply, secure in their heart
With an anchor that holds and can not pull apart.

What a joy is the family whose heart will stay true
To the call of the Savior, and will faithfully do
All the Master commands, of service and love,
Whose life here has purpose, whose home is Above.

Christmas Joy

In the Fullness of Time

In the fullness of time, He came
To a sin-weary world, Jesus came
To a stark manger bed, with no pillow for His head
But in the Father's great love, He came.

To a people in darkness, he came
In the stillness of night, Jesus came
While in the dark sky, shown a star up on high
And the Light of the Ages was born.

He came just for you and for me
This deliverer who would set people free;
For a people enslaved, depressed and depraved
He was a beacon for all who would see.

Let us join with the angels to sing
Of this gracious Redeemer and King
Once a baby He came, on the cross would be slain
So that all who receive Him will reign.

We Would Have Done It Differently

We would have chosen a palace
God choose a manger stall
To invade the world with His gift of love,
His redemption for one and all.

We would have chosen the powerful
Of the world to hear the song;
The announcement of the greatest event
In all ages to come along.

But it was only shepherds out on a hill
Who heard the carols of love
Who saw the vastness of angelic choirs
Filling the heavens above.

Who would have chosen a lowly birth
Or a simple maiden, unknown
To be the first to smile at him
On his strange little manger throne

And who would have chosen a desperate world
A world filled with sin and shame
To receive the most Unspeakable Gift
To bring life in one simple name.

It was God the Father who looked down in love
To a people, lost without hope
It was God who devised the humble plan
So far beyond human scope.

We would have done it differently,
But God in His wisdom chose this—
A starry night, an angel choir,
To shower the world with bliss.

And so we come on this Holy Night
In awe of the Father's design;
We kneel at His feet and thank Him for
The greatest Gift of all time.

The Light of the World

The people who walked in darkness
Have seen a great Light
A light that illuminates evil
And all that is truthful and right
Jesus, this Light, earthly born
In a Bethlehem stable so rude
An unfathomable Gift from the Father
Whose love our hearts will infuse.

And though the world still lies in darkness
And longs for the peace that he gives
May it reach for the Hope of the Ages
And rejoice that the Savior still lives.
Even now as we gaze at the manger
Let us join with the shepherds in praise
May we catch the sweet notes of the angels
As together our anthems we raise.

Where do you Stand?

This is the season of miracles—
A virgin birth by a young innocent maid
A journey during a late-term pregnancy
A long road to Bethlehem, David's town.

This is the season of adoration—
Wise men with their lavish gifts
Shepherds leaving their flocks behind
As they hurried to kneel at the manger bed.

This is the season of radiant light—
Heavenly hosts of angelic choirs
A brilliant star that appeared in the East
Guiding the wise men from distant lands.

This is the season of thoughtless rejection
There was no room in the village inn
There was no kindness in Herod's heart
No room in the hearts of the religious elite.

A Man who was good and kind and true
Bringing God's message of enduring love
Was rejected by those He came to save
And was spitefully hung on a wooden cross.

Now this is the season of thoughtful resolve:
We consider our place in this God-ordained plan
Will we adore? Or will we reject?
This marvelous gift offered to sinful man.

I Wasn't There

I wasn't there that beautiful night
When the angel throng lit up the sky
I didn't hear the wondrous song
As its heavenly strains wafted by.

But I know that once to this sin-battered place
Came a message of "Peace on earth!"
And I know that the only hope of each man
Was entwined with a Baby's birth.

I didn't see the brilliant new star
That led wise men from far distant lands
I didn't hear the caravan's hooves
As they plodded across desert sand.

But I know that their journey was not in vain
And the gifts they offered a King
Were gifts of honor and homage to one
Who caused thousands of angels to sing.

I wasn't there at the stable so rude
Where hay was the mattress of choice
And a young girl became a mother that night
I didn't hear her sweet voice

As gently and sweetly she welcomed her Son
The Creator of all that was
In her arms she held none less than God
Who is the Way, the Truth and the Life.

I wasn't there, yet somehow I see
How his humble birth only foretold
The salvation that came to earth that night
In a gift far more precious than gold.

And angels and shepherds and wise men are more
Than a story, a fable, a song
For God came to earth as a Baby one night—
Emanuel! To Him we belong.

Jesus Was Born for Me

Jesus was born for me one day
In a little Jewish town
It was only a stall with a manger of hay
But there God's love came down.
Wrapped in the humanness of flesh
Was the Son of God most high
Though perfect was He, a Spotless Lamb,
He was born that He might die.

My Jesus died for me one day
On a cross on Calvary's hill
It wasn't for crimes that He had done
But to do His Father's will.
He went to the cross for my sins and yours
For the debt that we could not pay;
Now a Holy God sees me through the blood
That poured down from the cross that day.
Jesus arose for me one day
And this message I'll sing loud and clear—
He is alive! He lives! He reigns!

He has conquered darkness and fear!
He was born, He lived, He died, He arose,
A victor o're sin and the grave;
His Name is worthy of honor and praise
He alone has the power to save.
Then one day this power touched my life
And I fell at His feet with tears;
As I worshiped Him whom my soul adored
And had sought for through long empty years.
Then there in that moment my heart was filled
I was baptized anew in His love;
Now He is my King, He's my Lord of Lords,
He's my Joy, He's my Peace from above.

Jesus will come for me one day
As a groom to receive His bride;
With joy I wait for Him to appear
Then forever I'll be at His side.
But while He tarries the Spirit calls,
While the Bride gently pleads, O come!
He'll save you, fill you, and heal you within—
Come let us adore God's own Son.
O come let us adore Him, O come let us adore Him,
O come let us adore Him, Christ the Lord.

Poems that tell a story

He Was His Own Man

They came in the 1920's and '30's
Not for the gold in the rambling hills
But for the gold that grew in the rich farm lands
Of California's great Central Valley.
They came with pockets empty and hearts full of hope
Because the West still called to the eager young man
Who saw his visions and dreamed his dreams,
Who believed in himself and the strength of his hands.

There were many who came, but not everyone stayed;
For some, the dream had too great a cost,
But others endured and worked and waited,
And finally the land was their own.

With pride they plowed and planted and pruned,
They watered and waited and reaped the crop:
The fields produced and the family was fed
And the spirit of the farmer was seen in his face,
In the spring of his step, and the set of his mouth—
He was his own man, and he had earned his own land,
No less a pioneer than the earlier settlers
He was part of a proud tradition.

They came, today, the mortgage holders,
And they pulled from the soul of the man and his sons
The land, and his pride and his dignity.
He lost the dream as he lost the land
But the nation's loss goes deeper still
For the heart of America is still the land
Her roots go back to the family farm
And the man who tended the soil—

He was his own man...he was.

Have You Heard About Jesus?

I was walking one day down a long dusty road
When I met a young man, on his back was a load
And I asked him to stop, sit and chat for awhile
For the noonday was hot, and he'd walked many a-mile
So we talked, and he told me that he had lost faith
In the goals of this world and the whole human race
Its people were hell-bent on money and fame
Caring not for each other, just making a name
He'd just gotten tired of it all and dropped out
Now he just wandered aimlessly, drifting about—
And I said, "Friend, have you heard about Jesus?"

I got in my car, drove downtown with a letter
I stepped out to mail it, and there in the gutter
Lay a wreck of a man, with eyes red and bleary
And as I smiled at him he began to get teary
And so, I sat down on the curb where he lay
And listened to the things that he wanted to say.
He's lost all his money, his good wife had died

His children were busy, they'd pushed him aside
His life had no meaning, his days were so long
If I'd give him the price of a drink, he'd move on—
But I said, "Friend, let me tell you about Jesus."

I stopped by an office to do business one day
And the businessman seemed to say, "Out of my way!
Can't you see that I'm busy, my schedule is tight,
With all of my work, I'll be up half the night!
I must catch that taxi, and get on the plane!"
And he barked out an order, both loud and profane
But I stood in his path, and I looked in his eye
This man who would someday take time out to die
Some day he would stop, someone else take his place
Who would hurry and scurry in his ceaseless rat-race—
And I said, "Friend, have you heard about Jesus?"

You know, it seems strange, as we go to and fro
The people we meet in this world here below
Whether housewife or doctor, rich man or bum
If they live in a mansion, or down in a slum,
How they simply exist, live in fear and in doubt,
With the foggiest notion of what life is about
Defeated and bored, disillusioned and sad
Confused so they hardly know good from the bad
When all the while Christians have something to say
That could change all that darkness to bright shining day—
It's just, "Friend, have you heard about Jesus?"

So, Brother, if Jesus is real now to you
Get up and get moving, there is something to do
We've got the best message that's ever been told
It is worth many more times the value of gold;
For the Jesus we know is the answer today
To the hard situations we meet on life's way.
There is nothing too big, there is nothing too small,
Whatever our need, we have only to call;
So, let's get out the message, "Friend, invite Jesus in
He'll give you new life, and He'll cleanse you from sin—
And my friend, you'll love Jesus."

In Conclusion ...

When I started putting this book together I had no idea how many poems I'd written through the years. But as I collected them, I became aware of various situations that had prompted one or the other, and realized afresh that many originated as thoughts that had spiritual significance for me. We all have a variety of thoughts and ideas about life issues as we go through life, but only the writer actually commits them to paper. I think there is a compelling force in some of us to write out our thoughts to see if they are significant or not, not to others, but to ourselves.

As I've gotten older, the power of my faith seems to grow. The tender spot that mirrors my love for Jesus, my Savior, becomes ever more sensitive. I am easily moved to tears. Today, one line was in my consciousness, snagging my thoughts throughout the morning, until finally I said, "Now where did I read that!" And finally I remembered—it was a line from a poem that read, "And I fell at His feet with tears." Did I write that, or where did I read that? Ah, yes—in one of my Christmas poems I'd written:

Then one day this power touched my life And I fell at his feet with tears.

And I worshiped Him whom my soul adored And had sought for through long empty years.

The date on the poem was 1976, and of course, I knew just what had moved me to write that line, because yes, that is what happened. One day the power of the Living Lord invaded my life in such a way that everything in my life changed. It would be the beginning of a walk with Jesus that has grown and matured in time, but the tears are never far away. Jesus loves me, without reservation. His grace covers my sin and my many mistakes and instead of judgment He offers me complete forgiveness, every single day. This is why the last verse states,

Jesus will come for me one day
As a groom, to receive His bride
With joy I wait for Him to appear
Then forever I'll be at His side.
But while He tarries, the Spirit calls
While the bride gently pleads, "O come!"
He'll save you, fill you, and heal you within;
Come let us adore God's own Son.

Blessings to you, my reader.
May you know His Peace.